SUCCESSFUL SELF-MANAGEMENT

Increasing Your Personal Effectiveness

Revised Edition

Paul R. Timm, Ph.D.

A Crisp Fifty-Minute™ Series Book

This Fifty-Minute™ book is designed to be "read with a pencil." It is an excellent workbook for self-study as well as classroom learning. All material is copyright-protected and cannot be duplicated without permission from the publisher. *Therefore, be sure to order a copy for every training participant through our Web site, www.axzopress.com.*

SUCCESSFUL SELF-MANAGEMENT
Revised Edition

Paul R. Timm, Ph.D.

CREDITS

VP, Product Development: **Charlie Blum**
Editor: **Michael Crisp**
Production Editor: **Genevieve McDermott**
Designer: **Carol Harris**
Layout and Composition: **Interface Studio**
Production Artists: **Nicole Phillips, Rich Lehl, Betty Hopkins**
Artwork: **Ralph Mapson**

Trademarks
Crisp Fifty-Minute Series is a trademark of Axzo Press.

Some of the product names and company names used in this book have been used for identification purposes only and may be trademarks or registered trademarks of their respective manufacturers and sellers.

Disclaimer
We reserve the right to revise this publication and make changes from time to time in its content without notice.

ISBN 10: 1-56052-242-9
ISBN 13: 978-1-56052-242-3
Library of Congress Catalog Card Number 91-72443
Printed in the United States of America

11 12 13 14 15 12 11 10

LEARNING OBJECTIVES FOR:

SUCCESSFUL SELF-MANAGEMENT
REVISED EDITION

The objectives for *Successful Self-Management—Revised Edition* are listed below. They have been developed to guide you, the reader, to the core issues covered in this book.

THE OBJECTIVES OF THIS BOOK ARE TO HELP THE USER:

1) Learn how one's positive personal behavior can affect others

2) Understand the application of personal values

3) Explore the use of feedback and help from others in self-management

ASSESSING PROGRESS

A Crisp Series **assessment** is available for this book. The 25-item, multiple-choice and true/false questionnaire allows the reader to evaluate his or her comprehension of the subject matter.

To download the assessment and answer key, go to www.axzopress.com and search on the book title.

Assessments should not be used in any employee selection process.

ABOUT THE AUTHOR

Paul R. Timm, Ph.D. is the author of eleven best selling books in the areas of management, communication, human relations, supervision and productivity. In addition to teaching at Brigham Young University, he also serves as president of The Blanchard-Timm Group, a firm that provides success coaching to thousands of people via seminars and related materials. Dr. Timm practices what he writes. He is the survivor of his own mid-career slump; he writes from experience.

PREFACE TO THIS REVISED EDITION

In the six years since I wrote *Successful Self-Management*, I've seen countless examples of people experiencing new levels of personal growth and life-satisfaction by applying these ideas. These people are breaking away from the ''do more, do better, and do it faster'' mentality that had them running like racehorses around a track that had no finish line.

From the millionaire computer executive who finds a new level of joy in teaching at a community college to the attorney who turns to woodworking or the homemaker who launches her own business, people are coming to their own definitions of success. Life, they are finding, is much more than reacting to the world's demands.

Success is being defined in a broader, more intelligent way. It is not what the world defines it to be. It is internally based and highly individual.

Regardless of one's definition of success, getting there is no accident. It is a process of self-management. This book provides a sensible, logical, and psychologically sound way to master self-management. With the skills you'll learn in this book, you will enjoy the thrill of the chase and the joy of reaching inner contentment that tells you that you are much more than a modern day racehorse. You are a person of enormous worth and potential.

Making the most of that potential may well be a matter of applying the keys to SUCCESSFUL SELF-MANAGEMENT. So let's get to it.

CONTENTS

P A R T

I

GETTING STARTED

Page 3 contains an assessment which will get you started on the path to improved self-management. It is essential that you answer each question honestly. Since **SUCCESSFUL SELF-MANAGEMENT** was designed as a ''do-it-yourself'' book, the only person affected by your answers and actions is you!

WHERE ARE YOU NOW?

Here are some important questions to get you thinking about where you are now...Answer each question honestly:

1. Do you have a clear picture of where you are going with your professional life in the next five years?

( ) yes ( ) no

2. Do others (i.e. your supervisor/subordinates) know about your plans?

( ) yes ( ) no

3. Have you set specific targets for your personal life for the next five years?

( ) yes ( ) no

4. Do those you count on for support (family, close friends, etc.) know about these targets?

( ) yes ( ) no

5. Are you totally satisfied with the progress you are making in your professional life?

( ) yes ( ) no

6. Are you satisfied with your personal life progress?

( ) yes ( ) no

7. Do you have a written method to track your professional and personal progress?

( ) yes ( ) no

8. Are your underlying values clear and sharp in your mind?

( ) yes ( ) no

9. Have you written them down?

( ) yes ( ) no

10. Do you sometimes feel guilty about successes you have?

( ) yes ( ) no

11. Are you as successful as you can be?

( ) yes ( ) no

SELF-MANAGEMENT DEFINED

> Your answers to the questions on the previous page can help pinpoint opportunities for self-management improvement. The balance of this book is designed to help you convert these "opportunities" for improvement into reality.

An acceptable definition of self-management would be:

"SELF-MANAGEMENT is the *process* of maximizing our *time* and *talents* to achieve *worthwhile goals* based on a sound *value system*."

Note the key words in this definition:

PROCESS: Self-management is ongoing: It is not something we do only once or occasionally. We make it a process by adopting some simple "rituals" which will be taught in this book.

TIME and TALENTS: These are unique personal resources which we alone can manage. In essence, this is all we have to offer and can really manage.

WORTHWHILE GOALS: These are the outcomes of our efforts—our planned-for achievements. To be truly worthwhile, such goals must be rooted in a sound value system.

VALUE SYSTEM: Ultimately, we move toward that which we value. Understanding our *personal* values is critical to the process of self-management.

As you work through this book, you will be taught the required skills to make the above definition of self-management a natural part of your life. In so doing, you will achieve even greater heights of psychological comfort and life satisfaction.

P A R T

II

FIVE
BUILDING BLOCKS
TO SUCCESS

FIVE BUILDING BLOCKS TO SUCCESS

The balance of this book will describe five "building blocks." Understanding and applying these concepts will allow you to develop the self-management skills necessary to become a more effective and confident person.

The five building blocks are:

BLOCK 1: UNDERSTANDING PERSPECTIVE

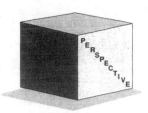

Perspective is our attitude about the amount of control we have over our lives. Some people feel helpless and overwhelmed by the demands the world seems to place upon them. Other people act as if they have virtually total *control* over every event that might affect them.

Let's think for a moment about this issue of personal control. I remember the first time I went skiing. My wife and I, both newcomers to the sport, visited a beautiful Utah ski resort with friends. After an hour of slipping around and feeling awkward, our friends Dave and Judy patiently explained the basics (i.e. how to stand up on the skis and create the illusion that you've done all this before). Finally they announced it was time to ride up our first lift.

It took only a few moments on the lift for a terrifying realization to enter my mind. I notice the lift seats were coming back down the mountain—empty. I also deduced that the lift never stopped to let people off! That meant that like it or not we were going to have to *ski* off the top of a mountain (to certain death, I was sure). The sinking feeling that we had given up control pushed us way outside our comfort zone. It was scary.

Some people feel they have no control over any aspects of their lives. They see themselves as helplessly floating on a sea of waves and currents. They resign themselves to drifting and that's exactly what they do throughout their lives.

Other people have unrealistic views of what they can control. They think that they have more power than they do and get very frustrated when people or events fail to yield to their control efforts.

Psychologists classify people according to their "locus of control."[1] Some have an *external* locus meaning that they see the outside world as controlling them. Others have an *internal* locus meaning that they feel they have a lot of control over what happens to them. An internal locus of control is needed for self-management although it must be tempered by reality. We are all subject to some external forces over which we have no control, but much in our life can be influenced by us.

---

[1] The term "locus" means place, locality, or source.

Like my wife and I on skis, we sometimes place ourselves in situations where we no longer hold control. Kids do this at amusement parks. They eagerly hop on scary rides. The more threatening the name of the ride, the better. The Maniacal Rodent, Terror Mountain, The Bone Crusher—they love them all. Other folks, when cajoled into riding one of these things, can think only of every possible way the ride could crash and burn. They hate giving up control even for a few minutes.

Although these conservative people may miss out on some of the fun, they take comfort in avoiding out-of-control feelings. In life, most of us grind against feelings of no control. In fact, a major source of occupational stress arises from having too little control on the job.

Off the job, people increasingly find themselves adding the number of balls they are trying to juggle. Career, family, civic or religious activities, physical fitness, education, and other self-improvement efforts all take a bite out of our precious time and drain our limited energy. This coupled with a "do-more, do better" mindset places considerable pressure on people. This is why many of us feel that our lives are out of control.

HOW DO YOU LOOK AT CONTROL?

HOW DO YOU LOOK AT CONTROL?

In the left column of the box below, list some events or activities which may affect your life, over which you have *no control*. (Typical items may be the weather or the stock market.) In the right column, list events or activities that you *can control*. Finally, list some events or activities that fit somewhere in between, in the gray area. These are things you may have *some* control over.

EVENTS OR ACTIVITIES THAT		
I CANNOT CONTROL	— GRAY AREA—	I CAN CONTROL

Do you see any common characteristics in the items listed on the facing page? Most people find that there are several things they cannot control and many of them have to do with **other people**. The activities in our lives that we can control usually have to do with **ourselves**. This leads to the simple conclusion that:

> THE MOST FERTILE AREA FOR GREATER CONTROL
> LIES WITHIN OURSELVES.

For most events in life we can have *some* influence—but seldom will we have ultimate control. This applies especially to our dealings with other people.

A healthy perspective toward life-control may be summarized this way:

Life is a never-ending series of demands upon our time and efforts. This "stream" is constantly fed by bosses, subordinates, family, friends, our sense of obligation, and our basic needs.

For the successful self-manager—one who tries to maximize control of his or her own life—the stream is also fed by clearly determined goals, aspirations, and values.

Look at who is feeding your stream. Then take control by choosing to respond to those demands that best meet your true needs. Herein lies the first key to successful self-management.

SELF-QUIZ AHEAD ⟩

SELF-QUIZ: HOW I ALLOCATE MY TIME AND TALENTS

Check yes or no beside each of the following statements to reflect how you act *as a general rule.* Be honest; don't show your answers to others.

1. ( ) yes ( ) no   I spend most of my day doing what other people want me to do.

2. ( ) yes ( ) no   I work on fun or pleasant tasks before doing the unpleasant ones.

3. ( ) yes ( ) no   I wait until a deadline is near before really getting to work on a project.

4. ( ) yes ( ) no   I give a high priority to those tasks that will advance my personal goals.

5. ( ) yes ( ) no   I tackle jobs that can be completed in a short time before working on larger, longer-term tasks.

6. ( ) yes ( ) no   I do the work which I've planned before doing the unexpected.

7. ( ) yes ( ) no   I tackle the small jobs before embarking on the bigger ones.

8. ( ) yes ( ) no   I work on the squeaky-wheel principle—the task that "makes the most noise" gets worked on first.

9. ( ) yes ( ) no   I wait to be told what to do first.

10. ( ) yes ( ) no   I regularly think about how I am expending my efforts relative to my personal goals.

SELF-QUIZ RESULTS

The self-quiz on page 12 may tell you something about your perspective on *control*.

If you answered YES to items 1, 3, 8, or 9 you tend to be REACTIVE to outside demand. You wait until someone (or someone's deadline) pushes you to action.

If you answered YES to items 2, 5, or 7, you may be acting upon MISTAKEN PRIORITIES. Your decision to work on something appears to be because it looks easy or can be done quickly. People who do this regularly find themselves *tangled in the trivial* and seldom seem to have time or energy for what may be much more important.

If you answered YES to items 4, 6, or 10, you are showing a PROACTIVE stance and are more likely in control. Saying YES to these questions means you are moving toward successful life-managment.

To be proactive is good, providing that you know where you are going. This brings us to our second success building block: PURPOSE which is described on the next page.

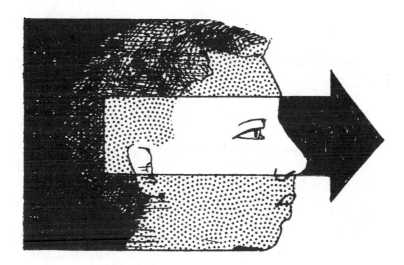

BLOCK 2: UNDERSTANDING PURPOSE

Our second success building block is PURPOSE. People without a strong sense of purpose lack focus in their lives. They are often guilty of living by wandering around *(LBWA)*, which may be the single most common cause of poor self-management.

Focus adds power to our actions. If somebody throws a bucket of water on you, you'd get wet, and probably get mad. But if water was shot at you through a high-pressure nozzle you might get injured.

Similarly, the "trick" to karate is that the entire force of a blow is centered in a very small area like the edge of the hand. That's why black belt karate experts can slam through a stack of boards with no pain. They are *focused*. No mental or physical "wandering around" here. The karate user's mind and body is totally concentrated, and the results are stunning.

Gaining Focus with Value Clarification or
Letting Your Bone Deep Beliefs Guide Your life

When Tom Peters, author of the well-known book *In Search of Excellence,* is asked for "one, all-purpose bit of advice" which will help organizations achieve excellence, he responds:

> "Figure out your value system. Decide what your company stands for...Put yourself out 20 years in the future: What would you look back on with the greatest satisfaction?[2]"

---

[2] Thomas J. Peters and Robert A. Waterman, Jr., *In Search of Excellence* (New York: Random House, 1982).

The same advice holds for individuals. Melanie Brown explains in *Attaining Personal Greatness* that "the real distinction between being great and being less great seems to be the extent to which we are willing to be pushed along *by our own best desires* [emphasis added]."[3] Clarifying and articulating these deepest desires isn't easy. If it were, more people would do it. It takes mental effort and some clear thinking. But once articulated, these true desires become the personal values that form the basis of successful self-management. This defines our life's purposes.

A value is a concept of the desirable—an idea that is, in and of itself, alluring. To make it a personal value simply add the words "to me." Clarifying a value system, for organizations *and* for individuals, is a powerful idea. Leading companies are aware of its power and we should be, too.

Your personal values need not be validated by popular vote. They don't have to agree with what other people think is valuable. They are uniquely yours. (Obviously if your value is counter to what society values, you may meet some resistance. If you value, for example, armed robbery as an expedient way to make a living, you'll pay a price for running against the norm.)

But on a more positive note, once our value system is clarified, it will provide focus for our lives. By contrast, less effective people and organizations are typically marked by no coherent set of bone-deep beliefs. They tend to look only at results that can be easily measured—*quantity* goals. They count how many of something they produce or sell, for example.

Value-guided people and companies, on the other hand, express their bone-deep beliefs in *quality* terms like customer satisfaction, innovation, personal growth, self-esteem and life-satisfaction.

The most important work of any leader is to clarify and breathe life into a value system. Once articulated, this system provides a mission statement for leaders and followers alike.

How can we identify our value system? An effective way to begin is provided in the worksheet on the next page.

---

[3] Melanie Brown, *Attaining Personal Greatness* (New York: William Morrow and Co., 1987), p. 17.

VALUES WORKSHEET

> Mark each of the values listed below in one of the following ways.

Put a check mark (✓) next to those values you personally espouse, or champion. These are values you would be **willing to dedicate significant time and energy to achieve.**

Put an X beside those values that you personally reject. These are values you would *not* be willing to expend much time or effort to achieve.

Put an 0 beside those values that are neutral to you—you neither espouse nor reject these.

Many of the values below will probably sound good to you. Force yourself to make some choices. Be honest about your willingness to dedicate a significant amount of time or effort to each. Do not show your responses to anyone.

I value...

_____ career success
_____ honesty in all my dealings
_____ religious activity
_____ social correctness
_____ open mindedness
_____ high individualism
_____ winning
_____ my family's success
_____ giving my children a competitive advantage
_____ financial wealth
_____ self-sufficiency
_____ involvement in government
_____ marital harmony
_____ fame within my profession
_____ being productive
_____ being creative
_____ serving the less fortunate
_____ health and vigor
_____ being law abiding

_____ being loyal to country
_____ orderly home life
_____ keeping all commitments
_____ knowing the right people
_____ having balance in my life
_____ having a wide range of friends
_____ having many skills
_____ being prepared for emergencies
_____ athletic excellence
_____ pride in my community, state, region
_____ musical excellence
_____ awareness of my heritage
_____ projecting the right image
_____ honoring my parents
_____ ability to build things

_____ habits of thrift
_____ accuracy of work
_____ strong discipline
_____ financial security
_____ personal attractiveness
_____ tolerance of others
_____ being witty, clever, articulate
_____ artistic sensitivity
_____ being a good team player
_____ dressing for success
_____ skill to influence
_____ skill to repair things or solve problems
_____ keeping careful records
_____ understanding other cultures— diversity
_____ being a leader
_____ mentoring others
_____ intellectual growth
_____ trust in God

Now rank order the four values you endorse most strongly and the four values you reject most vigorously:

My Top Four Espoused Values:

1. _____

2. _____

3. _____

4. _____

My Top Four Rejected Values:

1. _____

2. _____

3. _____

4. _____

The Value Worksheet is designed to start you thinking about values. Review your list of the top four values you support and the four you reject most strongly.

☐ yes ☐ no   Do you spend a major portion of your productive time moving toward agreement with your top four values?

☐ yes ☐ no   Do you spend time and effort moving toward achievement of values you *reject*?

In the box below, identify one value conflict you noticed from this exercise. Can you pinpoint areas where you are now spending too much time and effort? Are there other areas where you should be doing more? Suggest an action you could take to achieve better alignment with what you truly value.

FURTHER VALUE SHARPENING

This page contains another exercise that can help you begin to focus on your core values. Take a few minutes to answer these questions, bearing in mind that your responses will be just a rough draft. Then come back to these at another time and see if your answers still hold. Core values hold up to the test of time.

1. What would you best want to be remembered for? What will your obituary say about you when you have finished this life?

2. What are your most important goals for this year?

3. What are your major professional and personal goals for the next year? (Name two or three in each category.) For the next five years?

4. Twenty years from now,

    _____ Where will you live?

    _____ What will you be doing?

    _____ What assets will you own?

    _____ What abilities will you have mastered?

    _____ How will you spend your time?

5. If you had all the money you wanted, what would you do with your time? (Be specific.)

6. If you knew that you would die in one year, what would you want to accomplish?

MORE THOUGHTS ON VALUE CLARIFICATION

1. Values are crucial to personal excellence

Personal effectiveness and balance require us to hold a set of clear personal values. Without such bone-deep beliefs, we are much more likely to gallop off in different directions according to whim. Without values, self-management becomes little more than choosing from an array of equally worthy (or unworthy) activities. Without values, we become subject to "the tyranny of the immediate," and react to events rather than doing that which is most meaningful to us.

2. It isn't easy to sort out our values

If value clarification were an easy process, more people would do it. But it isn't and they don't. One reason for the difficulty of the task is that values often present conflicts between two desirable goods.

For example, a worker may feel a need to maintain friendships by socializing with coworkers, but this could conflict with the need to get away from others and finish a task. Another difficult choice may be the question of allowing children (or inexperienced workers) the freedom to make personal choices, which can result in the high cost of their mistakes due to inexperience.

Once values are clear, people reduce the need to make uncomfortable choices. Their behavior is spontaneously "right"—consistent with their values.

3. Value clarification must be put to work

Careful value planning takes time. This book will get you started, but the greatest benefit will come to those who spend hours on the *process* of value shaping.

One systematic way to do this is to set up a notebook[4] or planner that provides a place to write your core values and related activities.

THE 3-STEP VALUE SHAPING PROCESS

Using a "Life Plan Worksheet" similar to the one found in the Plan-It Life Organizer, let's work through an example of value clarification. Write your value shaping exercise on page 22 as you work through this exercise.

First, name the value. Give it a name that you feel comfortable with. A good value area might be called HEALTH AND VIGOR. Others could be FINANCIAL SECURITY, FAMILY, LEADERSHIP, PERSONAL SUCCESS, SPIRITUAL GROWTH or BALANCE. Use terms that are meaningful to you. (The activity back on page 16 shows many other possible names.)

Next, write the name of one value on your life plan worksheet in the left column (see example below), and after you have written the named value, *describe*, using the present tense, what it will be like when this value becomes a reality in your life—when you are living in agreement with that value. Following is an example using HEALTH AND VIGOR as a value:

plan·it life organizer | **Life Plan**

Core Values	Value Aligning Activities
HEALTH & VIGOR	
I exercise regularly and avoid harmful habits. I maintain reasonable weight. I get regular medical & dental checkups. I maintain vigor by daily planning, goal setting, and rewarding myself for accomplishments. I jog, play racquetball, swim, play golf, and occasionally do wild & crazy things to let off steam. I refuse to let stress grind me down. I avoid excessive worry. I view life as fun and full of opportunity	• Jog 1000+ miles this year • Get medical physical every 2 years • Have eyes checked every 3 years

Although the example shows all those descriptors in the present tense, it is not necessary to have achieved them all yet. For example, no one is always able to avoid stress or excessive worry, and perhaps some activities (such as golf) are not regularly played. But putting descriptors in the present tense indicates the direction that a person wants to go.

Here's another example, using the value heading FINANCIAL SECURITY:

plan·it life organizer	Life Plan
Core Values	**Value Aligning Activities**
FINANCIAL SECURITY	
I can afford all that I need, as well as some luxuries. I vacation with my family and with my wife each year. I have no debts; even my home is paid for. My income is secure. I have a plan for my retirement, adequate insurance, etc. I have good income — producing securities. We are comfortable, but not extravagant.	· Save 10% of earnings · Buy $5000 worth of Blue Chip, Inc. by Jan. · Review life insurance this year · Pay off auto loan within 18 months.

Following is a summary of the three steps in Basic Value shaping:

1. Name the value

2. Describe what it feels like to have this value as a reality in your life

3. Describe value-aligning activities—
   (These are covered in the next part of this book.)

plan·it
life organizer

Life Plan	

Core Values	Value Aligning Activities

Core Values	Value Aligning Activities

Life Plan	
Core Values	**Value Aligning Activities**

VALUE ALIGNING ACTIVITIES— THE COMFORTABLE MARRIAGE OF VALUES AND GOALS

Too often, people oversimplify setting goals. They confuse goal setting with wishing or daydreaming. It is much more than that. Goals rooted in clear values are the bedrock of any success program.

Much has been written about goal setting. We have all heard the familiar litany: set short and long term goals, concentrate on them real hard, direct your energies toward their accomplishment and you will have SUCCESS!

Goal setting is a motivational technique that works—it is not a fad. As one textbook which surveyed the research on goal setting concludes, ''In business and in life, goal setting is a uniquely powerful tool for increasing productivity.''[5]

But why does it work? It works because goals give direction to life. They provide points of reference

This book differs from many other goal setting books because it maintains that AT THE BASE OF ANY GOAL MUST LIE AN ANCHORING VALUE. Understanding the VALUE adds power to the goal.

If an individual sets goals, for example, to do the following:

(1) jog 20 miles each week

(2) take each of the children out for a ''date'' this month, and

(3) make 125 sales calls this month

what might be the underlying values? Write your answers in the spaces below.

1. _____

2. _____

3. _____

---

[5]Edwin A. Locke and Gary P. Latham, *Goal Setting: A Motivational Technique That Works!* (Englewood Cliffs, NJ: Prentice-Hall, Inc. 1984, quotes from dustcover.)

Author's commentary:

The jogging goal would probably be anchored in some value called health; the "date with the kids" goal would be based in a value having to do with family; and the sales call goal probably finds its root in a career value.

But goals often relate to several, interconnected values. The sales call goal can be based in financial, personal growth, or even social values.

A personal value system can be visualized as the foundation of a building. The goals and activities will be structurally sound only to the extent that the foundation is solid.

Failure to create a linkage between goals and their values runs the risk of working toward goals which have no permanent attachment to personal values. Such goals are hollow.

CHARACTERISTICS OF GOOD GOALS

Effective goals–the kind that really do motivate–should be

- *concrete and specific*–phrased in a way that is clear.

- *realistic*–they should stretch us, but not beyond the bounds of what is reasonable.

- *measurable in some way*–either we can count them (e.g., the number of miles run or items sold) or we can feel their accomplishment (e.g., reduced nervousness before people or more attention paid to the kids' needs.)

- *deadline-targeted.*

- *value-anchored.*

- *written*–an unrecorded goal is only a wish.

VALUE ALIGNING ACTIVITIES— THE COMFORTABLE MARRIAGE OF VALUES AND GOALS (Continued)

Go back to the Life Plan worksheets on pages 22 and 23. In the column to the right of the ''Core Value'' is a place to write your ''Value Aligning Activities.'' For each value you have described on the worksheet, write several such action targets which will help you achieve alignment with your value.

For example, next to the HEALTH AND VIGOR value on page 20, the individual has written that he/she will jog at least 1000 miles per year, get a complete physical exam every two years, have his/her eyes checked every three years.

In similar fashion, the FINANCIAL SECURITY value example on page 21 is accompanied by the following activities: Save 10 percent of earnings; buy $5,000 worth of Blue Chip, Inc. stock by January; review life insurance coverage every three years; pay off auto loan within 18 months.

Every goal-seeking activity in the above examples is anchored in a value. The value clarification process helps to make purposeful goals, and these goals provide the motivation to achieve success.

Herein lies the productive marriage of values and goals.

IF IT ISN'T WRITTEN, IT ISN'T A GOAL

People in my seminars often say, ''I have lots of goals, I just haven't written them down.'' My reaction: If a goal isn't written, it isn't a goal—it's a wish. Occasionally wishes come true, but not as often as goals.

The power of goals lies in the ways they plant ideas in the mind. To do so requires repetition. Repeated ideas reinforce the direction to go. Reading written goals provides the repetition.

ASSERTIVENESS QUIZ AHEAD

BLOCK 3: UNDERSTANDING YOUR PERSONALITY

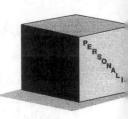

The third building block is PERSONALITY. While many aspects of personality can affect one's success, two aspects have the greatest impact:

1. ASSERTIVENESS

2. RECEPTIVENESS

ASSERTIVENESS

Assertiveness and aggressiveness are often confused. They are different. An excellent definition of *assertiveness* is **being pleasantly direct**. You need not be aggressive or pushy to be assertive. In fact, assertiveness creates none of the adverse reactions that aggressiveness or pushiness may.

Assertiveness calls into play the building blocks we've already discussed. With an understanding of CONTROL (Block 1), a clearer VALUE SYSTEM and FOCUSED GOALS (Block 2), you are now ready to make better decisions about the use of your time and talents. When faced with requests (or demands) to do something that runs against your plan, you'll have ammunition you need to say the most important word in the self-manager's vocabulary: NO.

With assertiveness, you will do so in a pleasantly direct manner.

HOW ASSERTIVE ARE YOU?

By honestly answering the following questions, you can get an idea of your attitudes toward assertiveness. An attitude, of course, does not always show up in behaviors. You may feel more assertive than you are in real-life situations.

Circle T (true) or F (false):

1.   T   F   I often feel like telling people what I really think of them.

2.   T   F   When I find myself in a new situation, I watch what other people do and then try to act the same as they do.

3.   T   F   I like to do things that others may regard as unconventional.

4.   T   F   I think it is important to learn obedience and correct social behavior.

5.   T   F   In general, I find that I dislike nonconformists.

6.   T   F   I prefer to listen to other people's opinions before I take a stand.

7.   T   F   I like to follow instructions and do what is expected of me.

8.   T   F   It often makes more sense to go along with "the group" rather than try to persuade them to my point of view.

9.   T   F   Confronting people is extremely uncomfortable for me.

10.   T   F   I enjoy being seen as a person with strong opinions.

SCORING YOUR ASSERTIVENESS QUIZ

If you answered TRUE to items 2, 4, 5, 6, 7, 8 or 9, give yourself one point for each. Also give one point for FALSE answers to items 1, 3 or 10.
Total your points.

If you scored 6 or more points, low assertiveness may be a problem for you. You may find yourself being far more reactive to the demands of others than you are to your own aspirations.

Many excellent books are available that can help develop one's assertiveness. Read some of this material and try on some new, more assertive behaviors.

HOW RECEPTIVE ARE YOU?
Receptiveness means fishing for Feedback

Getting feedback, even from your most severe critic, may be the most important way of gaining the direction and control that leads to better self-management.

While jogging together one afternoon, Terry and Marie got on the subject of corrective criticism. Terry confided that he was having some difficulty understanding why his career didn't seem to be going anywhere. He sensed that his boss wasn't very supportive—she didn't seem to care if he succeeded or not.

"If only she'd say what it is about me that doesn't appeal to her, I'd work on changing. But she just won't say."

"That can be frustrating," Marie agreed. "Maybe she's just uncomfortable telling you what bugs her."

"You're an old friend, Marie. What do you think I'm doing wrong?"

Marie thought for a moment: Terry is a really good guy, but he does have some irritating behaviors. For example, he's extremely competitive. So what the heck, she thought, I'll tell him now while he seems to be looking for feedback.

"Terry," she began, "You do have one behavioral trait that I find irritating, and maybe it bugs your boss too. You are the most blood-thirsty, competitive person I've ever met." Terry didn't say anything at first. In fact, he didn't see any inaccuracy in her statement, although she worded it pretty harshly.

In fact, Marie was warming up to this and Terry didn't seem too upset by what she'd just said, so she went on: "In fact, I notice whenever we play racquetball, it isn't even fun. You're so damn intense, you won't even say 'nice shot' when I hit a zinger. To be honest with you, Terry, you'd be a lot nicer guy to be around if you'd be a little more charitable with your compliments—a bit better at the old sportsmanship."

She was on a roll now: "In fact, Terry, I'd much rather play racquetball with Brent. Every game doesn't seem like life or death to him. He just has fun. And he's a nicer guy than you and he's forever saying 'great shot' and he's still a friend after the game even if I beat him and he even lets up once in a while if I'm really having a miserable game and...."

Suddenly, it sunk in that Terry wasn't responding. He wasn't getting mad and he wasn't even thoughtfully considering this ''constructive criticism.'' Actually he was laughing out loud. Marie found that disconcerting, until he explained:

''Marie, do you realize that you just described perfectly, *your* style on the racquetball court? That's exactly why I get frustrated playing against *you*.''

Marie wanted to give him her best ''Oh yeah, says who...'' when a large lightbulb went on over her head. He was right. She did do those things. Of course, she was just reacting to him. He started it!

After a moment, she started laughing too. He was right, of course. She was taking the game too seriously. But the exchange really was instructive. They both got some useful feedback and their friendship was strengthened by it.

Author's Comments on Terry and Marie's Conversation

Let's look at what happened between Terry and Marie. First, Terry asked for feedback from a trusted friend. That's receptiveness and it can be healthy. The story also illustrated that receptiveness can reveal interesting, and sometimes unexpected, information about both the participants. Both Terry and Marie learned something about their behavior as observed by the other.

What they each might choose to do with that information is up to them. In the interest of self-management growth, I would suggest that each has received a gift of a fresh perspective—a new look—at the way they may be coming across to others. This story also illustrates that sometimes receptiveness gets you information you didn't even ask for (and might not be all that eager to hear).

FEEDBACK RECEPTIVENESS QUIZ

Answer as honestly as possible. As a general rule:

1. ☐ yes ☐ no   I get embarrassed when people point out my mistakes.

2. ☐ yes ☐ no   I resent people who tell me what they think of my shortcomings.

3. ☐ yes ☐ no   I regularly ask trusted associates to comment on how I'm doing.

4. ☐ yes ☐ no   I offer constructive criticism to others in a sensitive way without hurting their feelings.

5. ☐ yes ☐ no   I like people who tell me how they react to my actions because it helps me do better.

Author's Comments on Feedback Receptiveness

If you answered a strong ''yes'' to items 1 and 2 you may be putting up some attitude barriers that could deter you from getting useful feedback.

We are all somewhat uncomfortable when we receive harsh or insensitive feedback, but even that can be valuable—if we take it in stride. Even our worst critic can give us a gift of good advice, if we don't allow the emotion of the moment to blind us.

Work to develop an attitude of searching for that gem of good advice, even if it's buried under a lot of worthless dirt.

If you answered "yes" to items 3 and 4 you are helping to create a climate where helpful feedback is accepted and expected.

Organizations with such a climate typically prosper. Likewise, individuals who foster an attitude of being ''teachable'' receive the benefit of the input of others.

If you answered a strong ''yes'' to item 5, you are probably a little unusual.

But you're on the right track.

We never really do know how we are coming across to others unless we ask—unless we seek some feedback. Feedback: the breakfast of champions—and a critical ingredient in *SUCCESSFUL SELF-MANAGEMENT*.

FEEDBACK IN BUSINESS

Why an Unhappy ''Customer'' Can Be Your Best Friend

Feedback is critical to an effective business. Customer service studies indicate that dissatisfied cutomers tell, on average, eleven other people about a bad service experience. Almost a quarter of unhappy customers tell 20 or more people. Studies also show that it costs five times as much to gain a new customer than it does to keep an existing one.

Another interesting fact is that most dissatisfied customers who receive some ''adjustment'' from the business do come back. The most dangerous situation is to have unhappy customers *not* tell the company of their dissatisfaction. In a sense, an unhappy customer is a company's best friend *if the company gets feedback.* Because of this, enlightened companies go to great lengths to make it easy for customers to complain.

Feedback receptiveness is an attitude. Less successful companies and people prefer to be ostriches. They bury their heads and tune out any negative comments. But they leave one end exposed!

Confirming and clarifying how we are coming across to others requires getting feedback from those we deal with. Feedback becomes the control system of our self-management.

Have the courage to ask, ''What am I doing that's stupid?'' (Well, maybe you'll want to phrase that a little differently, but you get the idea.)

Complete the following sentence in your own words:

I plan to encourage useful feedback by . . .

HOW TO NURTURE GOOD FEEDBACK

Remember, for most people, criticizing (even in a constructive way) is a risky business. When people first do it, they will watch very closely to see what happens. The reaction received usually determines whether such feedback will be given again. You can avoid turning off future feedback by:

1. **Staying nondefensive. Listen—don't explain or justify.** Learn to bite your tongue. This is not the time to explain or justify actions even when we feel the criticism is unwarranted or stems from a misunderstanding. When you ask for feedback, the burden is on you to listen and try to understand. This does not mean you are obligated to believe or accept the criticism, but try to understand why the other person feels and reacts the way he or she does.

   Defensiveness stifles the flow of feedback, for it tells the other person you are more interested in justifying yourself than in understanding him.

2. **Ask for more.** Especially in the open, verbal feedback process, there is an opportunity to get additional information. If you can honestly say, "That's helpful, tell me more—is there anything else I should know about that?" this will encourage the continual flow of feedback.

3. **Express an honest reaction.** The person giving the feedback often wants to know your reaction to the data he has presented. The best guideline is to express your honest reaction. "I'm a little surprised you said that, but you probably have a point." or "I'm not sure what to say. I never even thought of that, but I sure will from now on."

4. **Thank those who give you feedback and plan for the future.** Let people know that you realize how risky feedback giving can be and share your appreciation for their efforts. This might also be a good time to plan ahead for future feedback sessions, which should be less disturbing and more productive than the first one. Excellent leaders make this process a regular and ongoing one.

Now, having said all that about feedback, let me also say that not many people do this. Not because they wouldn't benefit from it but because they are afraid to. It takes a lot of guts not only to hear criticism but to actually fish for it! But then again there are many things most people would avoid to keep their heads comfortably planted in the sand.

The highly successful person is willing to do that which the unsuccessful person is not. Getting feedback which provides direction and control is a classic case of such an action. Dare to do it and you'll reap a rich reward.

FEEDBACK CHECKLIST

Think back to the last time you received criticism from someone else. Did you:

Yes	No	
___	___	Avoid defending or explaining yourself until the full criticism was expressed?
___	___	Understand the criticizer's point of view as best you could?
___	___	Ask for elaboration or clarification?
___	___	Express an honest reaction?
___	___	Thank the person for the feedback?

Get to the point where you can answer "yes" to these questions and you'll receive a lot of useful feedback.

BLOCK 4: UNDERSTANDING PLANNING

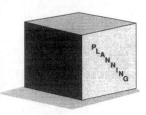

Planning is the fourth building block to successful life management. And it is critical to your success.

The Nuts and Bolts of Time and Task Management

Time management experts agree that rule number one in the planning process is this: *Use a planner.* I have designed a system called the *Plan-it Life Organizer* (you saw a sample "Life-Plan" page earlier). In the next few pages, you will see other sample pages from the Plan-It. You may prefer to modify your own planner system or use another format. But if you want to try the Plan-It, see the order form on page 52.

How much time should we devote to daily planning? I recommend a minimum of 10 or 15 minutes a day solely devoted to planning. Use the steps described below and you'll see a significant boost in your personal effectiveness.

How to Do Effective Daily Task Planning

Use the sample planner sheet on page 39 to practice effective daily planning. Here are the steps.

1. **Develop a priority task list for each day.** This helps sort out the important tasks from the less important. Determine which tasks need to be attacked first, and which can be saved for later or dropped entirely.

   Here's this process: List in your planner the tasks you want to spend your time on that particular day.

   Your list might include items like "Complete the XYZ report," "Get stamps," "Billy's softball game," "Eat more fish," or "Date" with your spouse or one of the kids.

   Don't be concerned with the importance of the items at this stage, just get in the habit of listing all nonroutine tasks that you'll want to do that day.

2. **Assign a letter priority to each item on the list.** Use A, B, C, or *(star). Put the letter A next to items that MUST be done. These are critical to you based on your values and goals. Tasks that are required, either by outside forces like your boss or by internal ones like your personal commitment will normally receive an A priority. (In the Plan-It, you place the letter in the column right next to the item. Put the letter A for MUST DO items.)

Use the letter B to indicate SHOULD DO items. These are things that should be done, items that would really be worth spending some time on. They aren't quite as critical as the As, but they are nevertheless important.

The letter C is used for COULD DO items. These are things worth listing, worth thinking about. And if you get the As and Bs all done, worth doing.

The asterisk indicates an item that is URGENT—something that must be done *now*. It is both important and time vital. You've got to get on it right away. The urgent task is not something planned during your dedicated planning time. It pops up and screams "do me now!" When these come up, add them to your list, put a star by them, and drop whatever else you're doing, even if it's an A item.

CAUTION: Use the star very sparingly. Be certain that an urgency is really important before you bump the rest of your plan to squeeze it in. Just because something makes a lot of noise doesn't mean it necessarily has to be done immediately. Don't let an apparent urgency override a planned *important* task.

Urgent items don't come up all that often. A, B, and C items should cover most of your tasks.

3. **Assign a number to these tasks.** You can further sharpen your plan of attack—your strategy for getting your work done—by assigning a number to each task.

Use the numbering system as a chronological indicator. That is, ask which task can I realistically get at first? If I have a meeting at two in the afternoon and it's an A item, it may not be A-1, simply because there are other things I'll want to do earlier in the day. You decide how you use it, but the number system provides your marching orders.

LET'S STOP AND DO IT...

Assume that tomorrow is Monday. Go through the three steps listed on pages 36-37 and prioritize what you really need to do tomorrow. Include both business and personal tasks—especially those that tie in with your core values. Write your plan on the next page.

Thursday

		Priority tasks	Schedule	Notes
√	A¹	Complete XYZ report		
→	C³	Get stamps		
X	B³	Call Bill re: wigits	8	
√	B⁴	Jog 5+ miles	9	Staff mtg.
√	A²	Get data for budget	10	
X	C²	√ with Harry re: golf	11	↓
√	B¹	Call Paula re: article	12	
Ⓗ	B²	Deposit check	1	
√	B⁵	Catch up on mail	2	
→	A³	Talk to Ray about billing	3	Call Bill re: wigits
			4	
			5	
√	A⁴	Billy's ballgame	6³⁰ Billy's game	
X	C¹	Read Lisa a story		

Friday

		Priority tasks	Schedule
		Mtg. w/ Carol	
		Date with Helen	
		Get Stamps	8
		Talk to Ray about billing	

YOU TRY IT

plan·it
life organizer

A	Must do	✓	Completed
B	Should do	→	Moved
C	Could do	○	Delegated
★	Urgent –DO NOW	✗	Deleted

Week of   19

This week

Monday

Priority tasks	Schedule	Notes
	8	
	9	
	10	
	11	
	12	
	1	
	2	
	3	
	4	
	5	
		✓ Journal ☐

Tuesday

Priority tasks	Schedule	Notes
	8	
	9	
	10	
	11	
	12	
	1	
	2	
	3	
	4	
	5	
		✓ Journal ☐

Wednesday

Priority tasks	Schedule	Notes
	8	
	9	
	10	
	11	
	12	
	1	
	2	
	3	
	4	
	5	
		✓ Journal ☐

UNDERSTANDING PLANNING (Continued)

Completion Symbols: The Payoff

As you complete the tasks listed in your planner, you deserve a reward. This reward takes the form of a completion symbol.

Here are several completion symbols, starting with one that feels the best:

(✓) The check mark symbol indicates the task has been completed. That, my friends, feels good. I prefer to put my check marks all in red just to remind myself of just how productive I've been, and how colorful.

(→) A second symbol, an arrow, is used when a task needs to be rescheduled, for whatever reason. Perhaps a meeting was postponed or an appointment changed, or the task simply could not be done because you were wrapped up in something else.

IMPORTANT: Any time you use the arrow, be sure to reschedule the task to another day in the planner. When you reschedule the task for another day, you earn the right to forget about it for awhile. It'll come up automatically on the new day you scheduled.

(○) A third symbol used is to actually put in the margin to the left of the completion symbol column a circle, indicating that a task has been delegated to someone else.

It may be that you've asked your spouse to pick up a book of stamps on the way home from work, or assigned Billy to clean out the garage before his ball game. Or, it may be a more formal kind of delegation, where you've given a secretary, or another subordinate, a task to complete. If you have several people to whom you delegate, you may want to use the circle and put the initial of the person to whom the task is delegated inside the circle. When the task has been completed by that person, you then put a check mark in the column.

(X) A fourth symbol is an X, which simply means that a task has been deleted. This may mean that you blew it and it just didn't get done, or it may mean that you've reconsidered and determined that this task simply isn't worth doing. Remember, you are in charge. If you schedule a task but later decide it really isn't what you want to do—so be it. You (X) it out.

Let's review the priority codes and completion symbols. What do the following mean?

A =   ✔ =

B =   → =

C =   ○ =

★ =   X   =

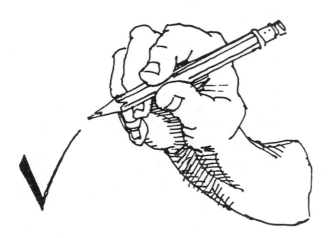

TYING GOALS AND VALUES TO YOUR DAILY PLANNING

Your priority task list provides a micro view of your daily activities. But how do these activities tie in with those long-term values and goals we've been talking about?

For most people they don't. And that's why people often fail to achieve what's really important to them. The challenge is to *make your daily activities consistent with your goals and values.*

In the *Plan-It Life Organizer©* you'll find three sections which give it special power to help you be successful.

1. A monthly plan section.

2. A yearly plan record.

3. Your life plan.

A sample of each of these pages is found in this book beginning on page 44. You may photocopy these for your personal use.

In doing your daily priority task planning, be sure that the goals and values you have articulated for yourself seep through. The "life plan" section of a planner is a place where you record your core values and your value aligning activities for frequent reference. The more often you review these, the more likely they will become real for you. When doing your daily planning, don't forget to review "the big picture" described in your life plan.

Likewise, your yearly plan and monthly plan should surface and become specific tasks on your daily activities. For example, let's say that your life plan indicates a high value placed on "health and vigor." You have then decided, as a value-aligning activity, you're going to get involved in a regular program of jogging. For your yearly plan record, one of your priority tasks for the year is that you're going to jog 500 miles.

You then translate that 500 miles jogging target into a task of jogging 60 miles this month. Put this goal on the monthly plan page. Since you have decided that you want to run 60 miles this month, you then need to translate that into daily activities. So your priority task now for a particular date may be to run three miles. Write that down, and in doing so, your values and long-term goals become daily tasks. You are focusing your energy on their completion.

Translate one of your core values into daily activity using the diagram below. Write one of your core values in the top space. Then work down to daily activities.

_____	CORE VALUES	"What are my lifetime goals?"
_____	YEARLY ACTIONS	"What do I want to accomplish this year?...every year?"
_____	MONTHLY ACTIONS	"What do I want to accomplish this month?...every month?"
_____	WEEKLY ACTIONS	"What do I want to accomplish this week?...every week?"
_____	DAILY ACTIONS	"What do I want to accomplish today to bring me more in line with my lifetime goal?"

PLAN-IT© FORMS

The next seven pages are taken from the *Plan-It Life Organizer©*. They may be copied for your personal use.

To be successful in the area of self-management will require some sort of personal planner.

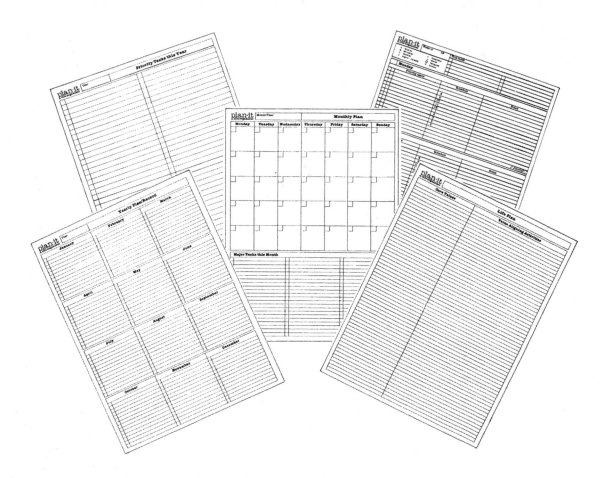

	Month/Year			Monthly Plan		
Monday	**Tuesday**	**Wednesday**	**Thursday**	**Friday**	**Saturday**	**Sunday**

Major Tasks this Month

plan·it
life organizer

Week of	19	This week		

A	Must do	✓	Completed
B	Should do	→	Moved
C	Could do	○	Delegated
★	Urgent — DO NOW	✗	Deleted

Monday

		Priority tasks	Schedule	Notes
			8	
			9	
			10	
			11	
			12	
			1	
			2	
			3	
			4	
			5	
				✓ Journal ☐

Tuesday

		Priority tasks	Schedule	Notes
			8	
			9	
			10	
			11	
			12	
			1	
			2	
			3	
			4	
			5	
				✓ Journal ☐

Wednesday

		Priority tasks	Schedule	Notes
			8	
			9	
			10	
			11	
			12	
			1	
			2	
			3	
			4	
			5	
				✓ Journal ☐

Thursday

	Priority tasks	Schedule	Notes
		8	
		9	
		10	
		11	
		12	
		1	
		2	
		3	
		4	
		5	
			✓ Journal ☐

Friday

	Priority tasks	Schedule	Notes
		8	
		9	
		10	
		11	
		12	
		1	
		2	
		3	
		4	
		5	
			✓ Journal ☐

Saturday

	Priority tasks	Schedule	Notes
			✓ Journal ☐

Sunday

	Priority tasks	Schedule	Notes
			✓ Journal ☐

plan·it life organizer | Year | **Yearly Plan/Record**

January	February	March

April	May	June

July	August	September

October	November	December

plan·it
life organizer

Year	Priority Tasks this Year

plan·it
life organizer

Year

Priority Tasks this Year

plan·it
life organiser

Life Plan

Core Values	Value Aligning Activities

plan·it
life organizer

Month/Year	Monthly Plan

Monday	Tuesday	Wednesday	Thursday	Friday	Saturday	Sunday

Major Tasks this Month

BLOCK 5: UNDERSTANDING PRODUCTIVITY

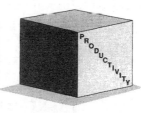

The last "P" of our success building blocks is "Productivity." Below are the six most common productivity killers. In the box next to each, list two or three defenses against it. Following this page I'll suggest some other ideas you may not have thought of.

Productivity Killer	What do you do to defend against this killer?

1. INTERRUPTIONS

   Is this a problem for you?

   (   ) yes   (   ) no

2. CLUTTER and PAPERWORK

   Is this a problem for you?

   (   ) yes   (   ) no

3. UNPRODUCTIVE COMMUNICATION

   Is this a problem for you?

   (   ) yes   (   ) no

4. PROCRASTINATION

   Is this a problem for you?

   (   ) yes   (   ) no

5. INDECISION

   Is this a problem for you?

   (   ) yes   (   ) no

6. SELF-OVERLOAD

   Is this a problem for you?

   (   ) yes   (   ) no

SOME TIME-TESTED DEFENSES AGAINST THE BIG 6 PRODUCTIVITY KILLERS

1. INTERRUPTIONS

> Assertively decline to be interrupted.

The next time someone asks, ''Hey, got a minute?'' you may be wise to gather up your most assertive skills—that doesn't mean being abusive or abrasive, but simply being assertive—and say, ''Gosh, I really don't. I'm in the middle of something right now. Could I get back to you in about 20 minutes?''

Do you think anyone would be offended by an approach like that? It's unlikely. But even if they are, the appropriate use of your time is more important than their momentary pique. Occasionally offering small offense to overly sensitive people is a small price to pay for greater effectiveness and satisfaction.

The most important way of avoiding unproductive interruptions is simply to *decline to be interrupted.* Tell people that you're working on something right now and that you'd be glad to talk with them later.

> Let people know when interruptions are okay.

Schedule particular blocks of time that are open for people to come and visit you with their concerns. Scheduling such time on your Plan-It, and coordinating it with your secretary, is a very useful way of letting people know that they can come in with problems they have during those hours. Then stick to those hours.

> Respect other people's time.

Don't interrupt others unless absolutely necessary. Always check with people to be sure they are not in the middle of an A priority. When calling on the phone ask, ''Do you have a minute to talk about this now?'' before launching into the topic of your call. By doing so, you send another unspoken message that you value time—theirs and your own.

> While you are thinking about interruptions, write at least one action idea you intend to apply to stop this productivity killer:
>
> _____
>
> _____

2. CLUTTER and PAPERWORK

> Handle each paper only once.

Learn to make decisions—not just postponing actions—on each letter, memo, or document you receive.

Usually you have four options:

> F–file it for future reference.
>
> R–refer it to someone else.
>
> A–act on it—now!
>
> T–trash it.

Studies show that 95% of the stuff in files for more than one year will never be used. Periodically clean out those files so that your system stays lean and efficient. When in doubt, throw it out. Get a handle on the kinds of information you need to keep and get rid of the rest. Don't get bogged down in sheer quantity of stuff cluttering your life.

> How to "read" a magazine.

As you read magazines, clip, or tear out items that are important to you. Set aside these articles, advertisements or other items that you may want to refer to in the future. *Do not keep the entire magazine*. Keeping the whole magazine simply adds to the clutter in your life.

By the way, about 75% of a magazine is advertising or information you don't need.

> While you are thinking about clutter and paperwork, write at least one action idea you intend to apply to stop this productivity killer:
>
> _____
>
> _____

SOME TIME-TESTED DEFENSES AGAINST THE BIG 6 PRODUCTIVITY KILLERS (Continued)

3. UNPRODUCTIVE COMMUNICATION

> Choose the right media for your message.

Don't send a letter when a phone call will do. Don't make a call when a personal visit is needed (even if the visit takes more time and energy). Communication *efficiency* is simply a matter of "reaching" the most people at the lowest cost. Memos, posters, and mass meetings can do that. Communication *effectiveness*, however, means reaching the right people with the right message in a timely and useful form. Often this means one-to-one conversations, small group discussions and the like. Effective communication media almost always cost more than efficient media. Many people, however, fail to count the costs of the backlash when efficient media is used inappropriately (such as a mass announcement of an issue that should have been handled personally).

> Keep getting feedback.

Even "simple" instruction giving should be accompanied with feedback. Always give the person you are talking to the opportunity to question and clarify.

A few extra moments spent now can save hours of "fixing" later.

> Keep your boss apprised of your priorities.

A five-minute planning meeting each day can clear the air and improve organizational productivity.

If your boss doesn't seem to be too open to such a meeting, try this: Each day, give your boss a brief memo saying something like this:

> Dear Big Boss,
>
> Here's what I'm going to be doing today. I've assigned my A-1 priority to finishing the Murphy report. When I'm finished with that, my A-2 priority is getting together the data for the budget [etc.].
>
> If these priorities are not consistent with what you need me to be doing, please let me know. If I do not hear from you, I will assume that I'm on the right track.

A simple memo like that provides effective communication and coordination.

> While you are thinking about unproductive communication, write at least one action idea you intend to apply to stop this productivity killer:
>
> _____

4. PROCRASTINATION

- Some experts say there are just three reasons for procrastination: fear of failure, fear of success, or the desire to rebel against "the system." Determine which reason you are using when you procrastinate a task.

- Use your daily priority task list found in your planner.

- Do the worst task first. Get it over with and enjoy the rest of the day.

- Make dreaded tasks into games. Compete against others or yourself. Try to beat your last effort. Play mind games.

- Discipline (sorry, but ultimately it may come down to that).

While you are thinking about procrastination, write at least one action idea you intend to apply to stop this productivity killer. (Do this now, not later.)

_____

_____

SOME TIME-TESTED DEFENSES AGAINST THE BIG 6 PRODUCTIVITY KILLERS (Continued)

5. INDECISION

- Successful people are seeing the value in the simple three-word motto, READY-FIRE-AIM. Think through your idea (get ready), try it (fire!), and observe/correct the results as needed (aim). Wal-Mart founder Sam Walton bought into this approach when he constantly challenged his people to try out new ideas, not just mull them over in their minds. Get yourself *doing something* and then adjust the aim as necessary.

- Avoid "perfection paralysis." Everything you do won't be right, but start with "rough draft" and shape and improve as you go.

- Decide to be more decisive. Make your decisions and stick to them so long as they still make good sense.

> While you are thinking about indecision, write at least one action idea you intend to apply to stop this productivity killer:
>
> _____
>
> _____

6. SELF-OVERLOAD

- I've talked throughout this book of ways of focusing your energy on things that are important—the value-based things that are important to you. A constant focus on the valuable is critical to reducing the problem of self-overload. If a task doesn't add value in some way, don't do it.

- Delegate all you can, not just what you want to. Be creative in seeking ways to double up your efforts with other people's. Offer to help when they need it and they'll be there for you.

- Put your major efforts into your value-based activities. (The other stuff isn't as important.)

- Stay flexible. Don't become a time nut. Someone described a time nut as one who got so programmed that he missed a slot in a revolving door and it threw him off for a whole week.

  If you get off stride, if you forget to use the planner for a day or two, or if you forget to use some of these other techniques, don't worry about it. Just step back and start over again. But once you develop the habit of using these tools, you'll find that you'll achieve a stress-reduced balance in your life.

  Don't become a robot. Understand the nature of time and these principles of self-management but stay flexible.

DECISION GUIDE

When deciding how to use your time, ask:

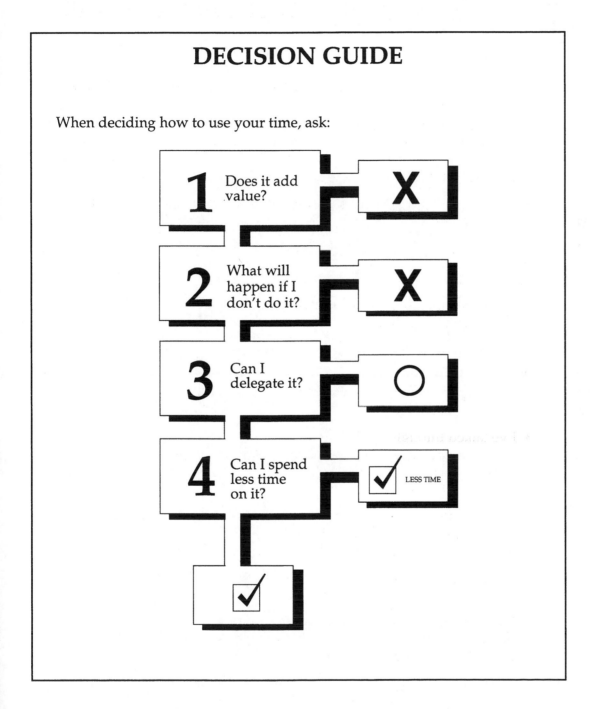

P A R T

III

A FINAL THOUGHT ABOUT BALANCE IN YOUR LIFE

A FINAL THOUGHT ABOUT BALANCE IN YOUR LIFE

Tony's story:

Tony sure looked successful. He was a young executive with a fast-growing company. His work seemed exciting. He traveled quite a bit (always first class), earned a salary that put him in the top 10 percent of wage earners nationally. He drove a sporty car, wore an expensive watch and dressed sharp. He was the kind of guy a lot of college students aspired to become. He had it made.

And he was miserable.

Under the thin veneer of success lived a basically unhappy man—a fellow traveling life's fast lane with a seriously lopsided wheel. Tony's problem was one of balance.

His career had become his whole life. He loved his job and dedicated himself to it with a vengeance. But after work, there wasn't much else to life. Tony was single and had no regular companionship with people who cared about him away from the office. His family lived halfway across the country; he was a member of no civic organization, no church, no nothing. His job was his life.

Lots of people fall into the lopsided wheel trap. We get wrapped up in some aspect of our life (career, kids, church work, civic involvement, physical training, politics, whatever) so deeply that nothing else is significant. We become compulsively one-sided.

WELLNESS AND CENTERING A LOPSIDED WHEEL

How do we achieve a sense of wellness—a social and psychological as well as a physical sense of well-being? A centered wheel can help.

Visualize an old-fashioned wheel with spokes. If the spokes are all about the same length, the wheel is balanced. If not, we're talking bumpy ride.

Everyone's wheel has a different number of spokes. The minimum number is three, representing values such as:

- Our PERSONAL life (including our sense of growth, spiritual dimensions and psychological and physical well-being),

- Our RELATIONSHIPS (including the well-being of our family, friendships and rewarding social involvement),

- Our CAREER (or avocation: the efforts we make to produce or create something of value and receive the rewards associated with that).

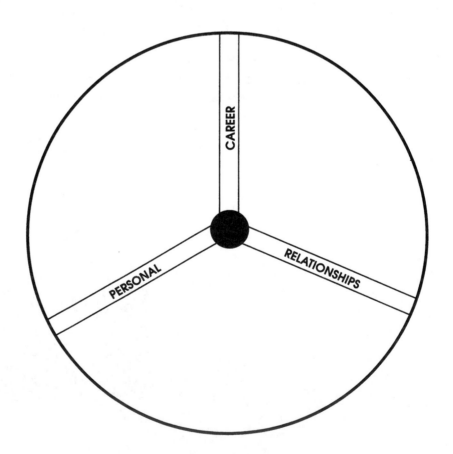

Some people envision wheels with more spokes, like the one below. Each spoke represents a growth dimension of life——sources of satisfaction or dissatisfaction. Use your own core values as spokes. For example, yours might include:

1. Physical

2. Mental

3. Career/Financial

4. Spiritual/Service

5. Family/Social

6. Value Congruence

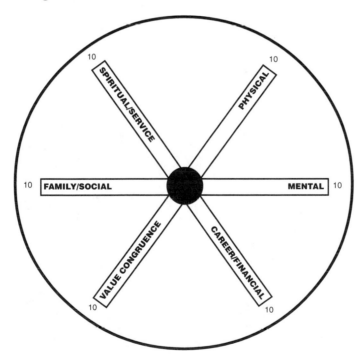

The centered wheel above is an example of good life-balance. Each spoke on the wheel is calibrated from zero to ten, representing your *degree of satisfaction* with the *progress* you are making toward value congruence. A one reflects extreme dissatis-faction; a ten, a feeling of great satisfaction.

A LOPSIDED WHEEL: AN EXAMPLE

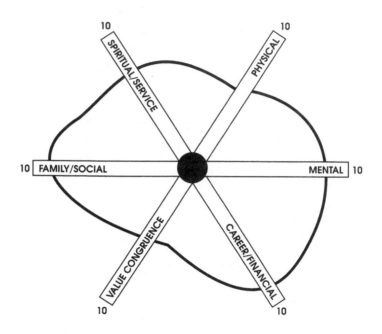

The wheel above is an example of a lopsided wheel. Although spokes such as FAMILY/SOCIAL and CAREER/FINANCIAL suggest feelings of rather high satisfaction, other spokes, like VALUE CONGRUENCE, indicate areas of lesser satisfaction. The lopsided wheel helps show you specifically what areas to work on to reach a better balance.

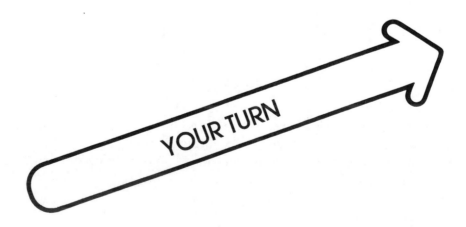

YOUR TURN

IS YOUR WHEEL ROUND OR LOPSIDED?

Now determine your own state of life-balance. Label each of your spokes from one to ten. Then draw a line connecting the points on each spoke. Is your wheel lopsided? Is it square? Is something sticking out too far?

Look at the short spokes and determine what can be done to boost your satisfaction with those aspects of your life.

Redraw your wheel every month or so. (An extra copy is found on the next page.) By doing so, you can achieve a sense of balance—the feeling that comes from using time and resources to gain satisfaction in the areas that are critical to whole person wellness. That is the essence of successful self-management.

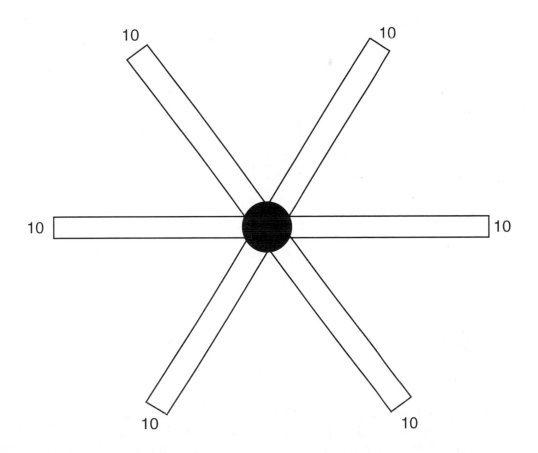

YOUR BALANCE WHEEL

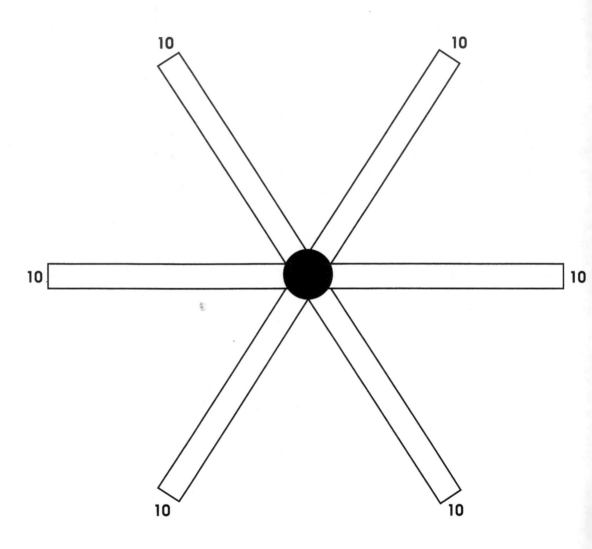

Rate the progress you are making towards congruence with your core values.
Name each spoke and then rate yourself from 0 to 10. Feel free to add additional
spokes to represent other values. Then draw the wheel connecting your spots on
each spoke. Do this every few months in a different color ink to see what kind of
progress you are making.